Self-defense and self-assertiveness

for women and girls

AF187025

Jens Müller

Self-defense

and

self-assertiveness

for

women and girls

Fighting right gives you the might

Books on Demand

**Self-defense and self-assertiveness
for women and girls**

**Bibliographical information of the "Deutsche Bibliothek"
[German National Library]:**
The "Deutsche Bibliothek" lists this publication in the
"Deutsche Nationalbibliographie" [German National
Bibliography]; detailed bibliographical information is to be
found on the webpage:
http://dnb.ddb.de

© 2018 by Jens Müller

Photo credits:
All photos and photo processing:
Detlef Sundermann, photojournalist

Translation:
V. J. Herrera

Making and publishing:
BoD- Books on Demand, Norderstedt
ISBN 978-3-7481-5002-2

Contents

Preface

This book shall serve women without experience in martial arts as means and manual to be effectively prepared to defend themselves against harassments or assaults of any kind.

Techniques have been chosen which are fast and easy to learn and do not require many years of training in the martial arts.

Throwing techniques have deliberately been left out, taking into account the fact that women generally are smaller, weigh less and have less strength than men.

This disadvantage is being compensated by the high efficiency of the techniques so that even a slender woman can defend herself against a taller, heavier and stronger man.

A key factor which cannot be covered even by this book should not be forgotten:

Practice makes perfect.

Only frequent practice and constant repetition can guarantee a fluid and instinctive performance of the techniques and movements.

Jens Müller   October 2018

The author

Jens Müller, born 1964, started judo at the age of eight. He was successful at competitions, holds the fifth dan (black belt) and owns a license as youth coach.

Furthermore he has been practicing Shotokan Karate for more than 20 years and Ninjutsu as well as Modern Self Defense (MSD) for 15 years. The author also has skills in Jujutsu, Tantojutsu (knife fighting) and Aikido.

The author worked as judo coach for children and adults for more than 20 years and as karate coach for children for about 10 years.

Due to his broad knowledge of the martial arts Jens Müller, in 1987 started developing self-defense courses meant especially for women. These courses are composed of the above mentioned martial arts systems practiced by the author.

For years he taught these self-defense courses at an adult education center in the Rhine-Main area.

The author works full-time at a bank in Frankfurt am Main. He stopped working as a youth coach but dedicates his free time to self-defense for women and is himself still an active martial artist.

Jens Müller is married and has one son. He lives with his family near Frankfurt am Main.

Legal basis

Self-defense § 32 StGB

(1) A person who commits an act in self-defense does not act unlawfully.

(2) Self defense means any defensive action that is necessary to avert an imminent unlawful attack on oneself or another.

§32 (2) also talks about the possibility of a defensive action for another. This would then be defense of others.

Excessive self-defense § 33 StGB

A person who exceeds the limits of self-defense out of confusion, fear or terror shall not be held criminally liable.

As an excessive self-defense you have to count a defense which exceeds the pure defense of an attack.

These are excerpts of and comments on the German law, other countries have differing legal basis.

Self-assertiveness

Every human being knows fear. Some more, others less. Fear in principle is not necessarily negative, as it is meant to warn us of dangers.

There are many types of fear: agoraphobia, exam nerves, the fear of losing one´s job, the fear of using an elevator, acrophobia, etc.

And it is completely normal for a woman to feel frightened when she is being molested or even attacked. This fear needs to be overcome otherwise you are pushed easily into the role of victim, a role hard to emerge from.

To escape the role of victim it is necessary to deal with fear first.

So how do you learn to handle your fear?

First you have to accept your fear, face it, fight it and then overcome it.

Your mental attitude is crucial. "Faith can move mountains". This is a well-known quotation. Well, maybe faith cannot necessarily move mountains but the core of this statement has surely something to it.

One should deal with a situation beforehand and be mentally prepared for it. Then you will not be caught off guard.

An example:
Let us assume a plank, about 20 inches wide and about 10 feet long, is lying on the floor and a person is asked to walk across this plank. No problem that is an easy thing to do. Now let us assume the same plank is not lying on the floor but on two tree

trunks which are 16 feet high and the person is given the exact same task. Is it still no problem?

Why is it a problem now? It is still the same plank, nothing changed besides the height. But this is exactly the point, because you start to think about all the things that might happen.

It is precisely the same in self-defense. You have to get involved in it mentally and prepare yourself. You must want to defend yourself.

Every woman takes her own decision whether she wants to defend herself. Once she has decided to do so she has to stick to it uncompromisingly because only with an inner attitude like this she will succeed.

If she defends herself only halfheartedly, the most crucial requirement is missing and the probability of a defeat rises.

Of course you do not need to go all the way and kill the aggressor but you have to put him out of action. If he is still able to attack you for a second time, you will probably not stand a chance, because the attacker will now be even more aggressive, more brutal and more unscrupulous than the first time.

Every human being has got a personal distance zone. You may observe this for example in a doctor´s waiting room. If there is one patient already sitting in the waiting room and another one enters, this second patient will usually not sit right next to the first patient but will leave one or two seats empty before sitting down at a distance.

This can be explained with the personal distance zone which is also of great importance in self-defense.

For example if a lady walks through a park or a lonely area in the dark, she will instinctively notice another person coming too close and entering her personal distance zone. If the other person passes in an adequate distance, this will not be seen as threatening.

So listen to your feelings and instincts.

Another example:
Every night you walk through a dark neighborhood without feeling frightened. But one night it is different. For some unexplainable reason you are scared or at least have a very strange feeling and you do not want to take your usual route through this dark neighborhood. Then don´t do it! Opt for another route or another mode of transport this night. Some women have the so-called sixth sense i.e. they have premonitions. Maybe you can take your usual route again the next day without the least bit feeling scared.

Conflicts can also be avoided through nonverbal behavior. There is for example the "typical type of victim". These women walk with their heads bowed and their shoulders hanging. They look down to the ground, walking closely to a wall and often look around nervously. This behavior or this radiance respectively is naturally easy to recognize for a potential aggressor and thereby he has already chosen his victim.

I now come back to the above mentioned. Occupy yourself with the situation beforehand. If you need to walk through a dark neighborhood, give thought to the path you want to or have to take beforehand. Do not show any fear even if you are frightened. A potential aggressor does not need to know that and least of all see it right away. It is ok to act a little bit. Walk with firm steps, look straight ahead, your shoulders upright. If you hear steps behind yourself, you may stop and turn around, but look deadpan. There is no one-size-fits-all approach, but sometimes it can make sense to address a person following you: "Hey, you`ve been following me for quite a while, anything wrong? Can I help you?" If you look directly at the person in question, keep the eye contact and clearly signal determination, this may already be enough to clarify the situation or defuse it. Or you stop and let the person pass by while you might for example look for something in your handbag or make a call with your cellphone.

A hint:
Do not shy away from dialing the emergency number [That would be the 110 for the police in Germany or the 911 in the USA]. Emergency services and the police are there to help in such cases!

This has been confirmed to me explicitly by German police officers with whom I work together in my self-defense classes.

It also makes sense to notify your whereabouts. That means if you have to walk home from somewhere, call a person of your trust and say that you are on your way. Or tell the person you are leaving you will call once you have arrived home. So the person informed could call the police when not hearing from you in the appointed time.

If you feel threatened by someone on your way home, change to the other side of the street. Then observe what happens. Does the other person also change sides? Then just change the side again. Keeps the person following you, you should take steps to defend yourself (i.e. address the person in question, address other people who might be close by, call help via your cellphone or the like).

When you drive your car in city traffic, lock the doors, by doing so you avoid the driver´s or passenger door being opened and you receiving an unwelcome visit.

But, like already mentioned above, there is no one-size-fits-all solution. Each situation is different. You cannot really practice an emergency, as, naturally, in an emergency you will be excited, scared and stressed out.

In a street fight there are no rules hence there is no fairness. So everything is permitted.

How you can defend yourself in case of emergency, you will read and see on the following pages.

Shock techniques

The interception into your opponent´s attack and a counter attack may sometimes turn out to be problematic because of the superiority in strength of the aggressor. So it is a good idea to always start your counter attack with a "shock technique" or diversionary tactic.

This means you need to divert the aggressor form your main tactic. You can do this for example by screaming at the aggressor. The so-called "kiai" (battle cry) has different objectives. For one thing it helps the person threatened to reduce the fear she will definitely feel in such a stressful situation. For another thing the cry will irritate the aggressor for about 1-2 seconds and you have to exploit this short amount of time to apply your defense technique. The kiai may also – depending on situation and local conditions – call the attention of passersby to the incident and these people may then help you. But you should never count on the help of others as passersby very often just watch the incident from a safe distance. But if you worked this book through thoroughly, you will not need any help as you will be able to clarify the situation all by yourself to your advantage. Other "shock techniques" or "diversionary tactics" are for example a kick against the aggressor´s shin, a step onto his foot and so on.

Position to the aggressor

It is not recommendable to stand head-on to the aggressor, because like that you offer the greatest possible room for attack.

It is much better to position yourself sideways to make the room for attack as small as possible.

Sometimes you may not have the opportunity to position yourself sideways. But even when you stand head-on to the aggressor there are some postures from which an attack is possible as well as a defense.

On this photo you can see that the weight is entirely put on the back leg, so you can perform kicks with the leg in front.

You can parry a blow to your head or your body without difficulty with your left arm. As counter-attack a kick with the foot e.g. would be useful.

Furthermore it is of great advantage to use your own body weight to enhance the efficiency of your own technique. This shall clarified by the example of a push. In the first example a person is being pushed just with the arm, without using the body's weight.

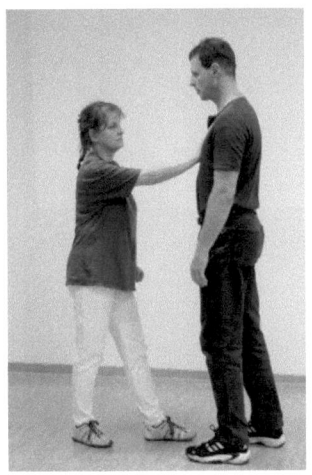

But in the second example the own body weight is being used in the push. You can see clearly that the effect of the push is much higher now.

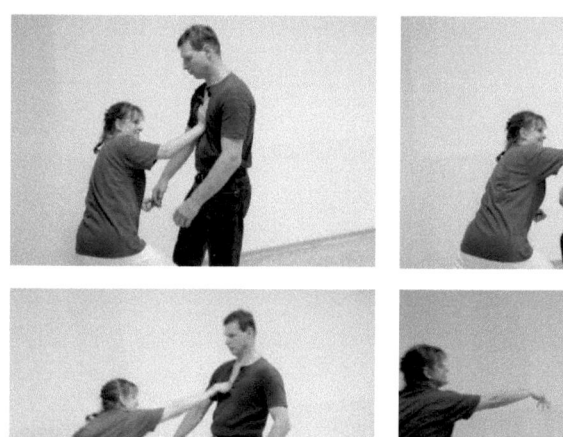 

Defense against harassment

Some techniques against harassment are shown below. These techniques are relatively harmless, but very effective.

Thumb crush

This is a defense against a hold of the lapel. The thumb of the attacker is being crushed. You do this by grabbing the second phalanx of the attacker´s thumb with your index finger and thumb and then squeeze it. The top (the first phalanx) of the thumb is being pressed backwards towards the attacker´s wrist.

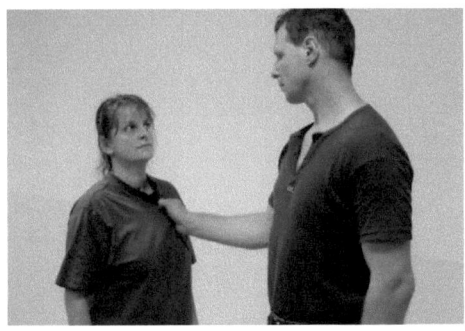

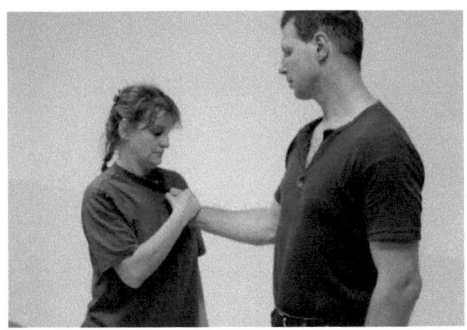

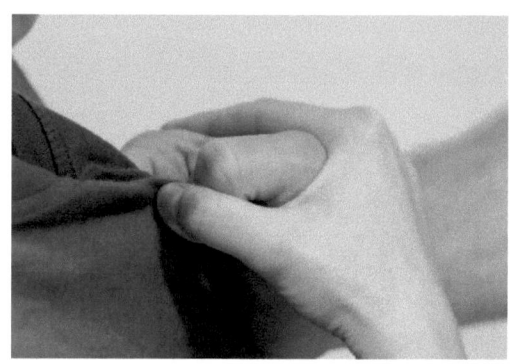

24

Multiple shin kick

Step onto the attacker´s foot or kick his shin. You may also do this in kind of a chain reaction i.e. first you kick one of the molester´s shins, when he steps back in pain you kick his other shin so that he will go one step back again. Then you kick again the shin in front and so on. Like that you can drive the attacker in front of yourself until he decides to flee.

Finger jab to the trachea

Another very effective method is to jab your index and middle finger into the trachea (the hollow below the larynx) of the aggressor and to push him back.

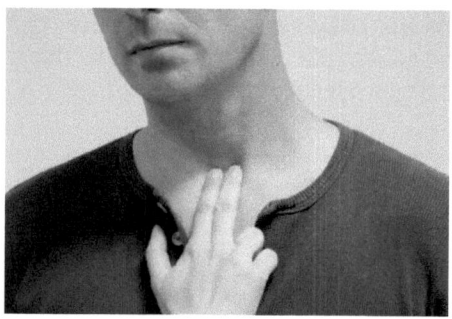

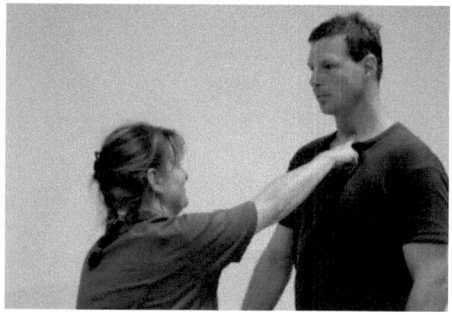

The fist
In self-defense it is crucial to clench a fist. This counts when
you fend off an attack as well as for your own counter attack.
In the following the proper formation and position of the fist
will be explained.

You start to roll your fingers beginning at the little one. Then
you put the thumb in front of the fingers to protect it from
injury. The thumb is by no means inside the fist because this
may lead to injury of the thumb or the joint capsule.

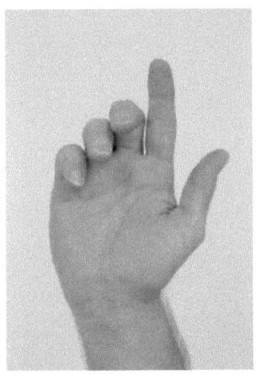
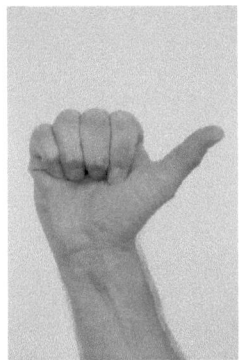

For the sake of clarity it is mentioned that normally the hitting surface when doing a fist punch are the two knuckles sticking out the furthest i.e. the knuckles of the index and the middle finger.

Like already mentioned in the theoretical part, there are no rules in self-defense or street fighting. So in an emergency it does not matter with what you hit as long as you hit.

You can practice first punches on soft objects like a pillow, a couch, a matrass and so on. If you are willing to invest a few euros or dollars, you may also purchase a punching beag or a punch cushion ("makiwara") in a sports shop.

The defense

Defense by forearm block is none of the most often used defense techniques. That is why we look upon it in greater detail. Experience shows that women tend to execute the defense by forearm block too weakly and softly. This means that the defense is without effect and the attack has achieved its goal. But this is what needs to be prevented. The defense of a strike (a forearm block) needs to be carried out as resolutely and with the same amount of power as a counter attack. The best way to do this is by clenching your fist. By doing so you flex your forearm muscles, something that will not happen if you perform the forearm block with your hand open because then your muscles are relaxed. So it is much more effective to also clench a fist before performing defense techniques.

The power resulting from the impact of the arms of attacker and defender is so enormous that this can very well lead to injuries. This risk of injury is being reduced through the fist and the thereby flexed muscles.

In the following you can see some variations of the forearm block.

Upward forearm block

Forearmblock to the middle from outside to inside

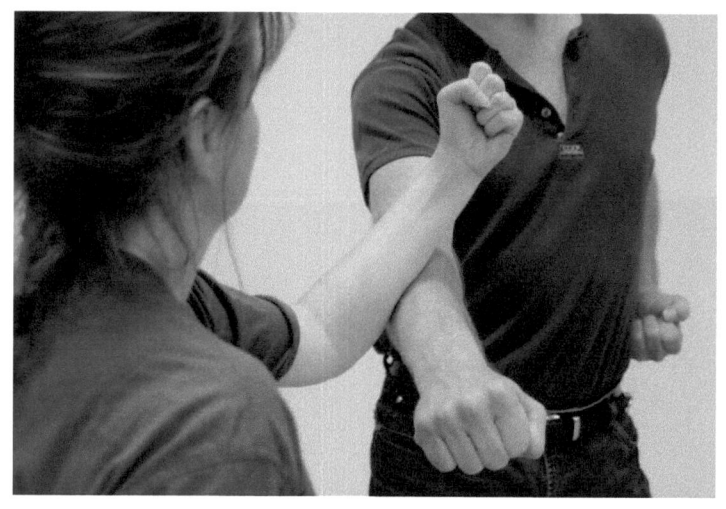

Downward forearm block from outside to inside

Defense against a blow to the head (swing, slap in the face or the like)

You are standing sidewards to the attacker in defensive stance. Your hands are already clenched to fists. Ideally the defense takes place in parallel i.e. when the aggressor attacks with his right hand the attack is being defended with the left arm (upward forearm block); immediately thereafter follows the counter attack with a fist punch to the nose (fracture of the nose bone) or to the chin; directly afterwards you perform a kick to the genitals whereupon the aggressor is incapacitated. The defense and the counter attack should be performed with a combat shout (shock technique). The order of the two techniques of counter attack is interchangeable of course. So you can perform the kick to the genitals first and thereafter the fist punch.

To fend off the capture of a sleeve or the shoulder

The aggressor grabs you by the sleeve. Defense starts with a strike to the aggressor´s biceps (you do this with the arm that the attacker is grabbing). Thereafter you put your arm from the top onto the elbow of the attacker. Then you perform an armlock, you do this by moving your arm forward. At the same time you kick the leg (back of the knee or calf) of the aggressor with your foot. The aggressor goes down. More kicks and punches should follow to incapacitate the attacker.

 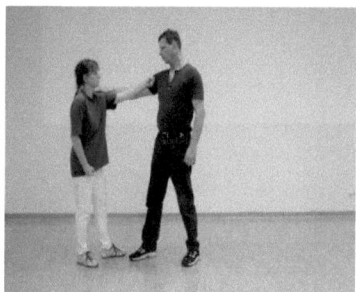

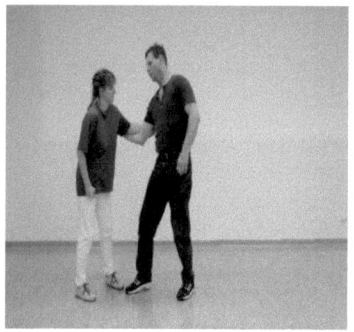 

 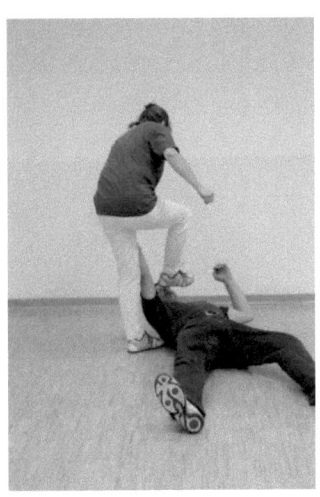

It is another possibility to not put your own arm from the top onto the elbow of the attacker, but to come from below. Your hand reaches the shoulder of the attacker. Essential for the success or failure of this technique is that you put your arm behind (seen from the defender´s perspective) the elbow of the attacker that is how you get an armlock. At the same time you have to fasten the attacker´s hand with your other hand to prevent the attacker from letting go and thereby escape the counter attack. The attacker bends forward to relieve the pain coming from the armlock which will give you the opportunity to kick him either in the upper body or the face.

Defense against a chokehold

From the front

If somebody is choking you from the front the distance to your aggressor is very short. Normally he will choke you with bent arms as you have more strength in bent arms than in outstretched arms. The short distance makes defense easier. First you do a knee strike to the genitals. Right thereafter follows an attack to the face of the aggressor; either a finger jab into the eyes or a strike with the heel of the hand onto the aggressor´s nose. This strike leads to a fracture of the nose bone, whereby the attacker is disabled. A fracture of the nose bone comes with severe pain and a great amount of bleeding. But you may always opt to add a punch to the head with your elbow or fist - just to make sure.

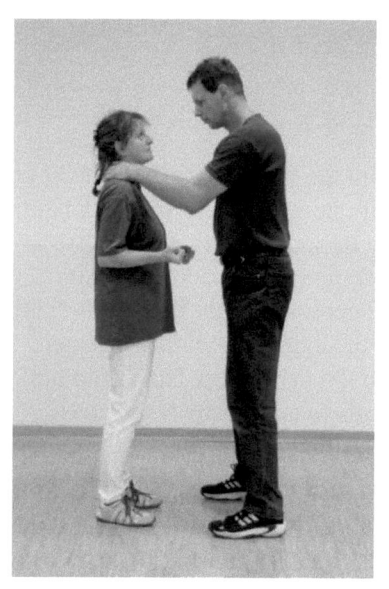

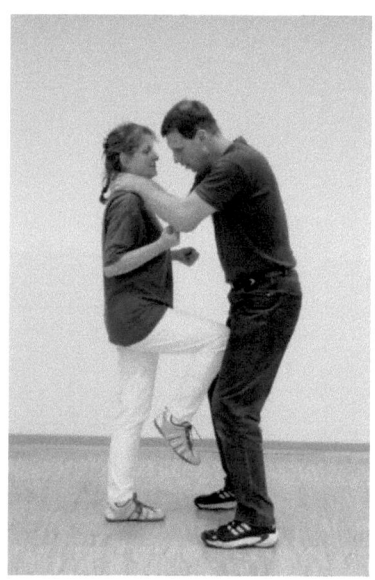

From behind with bent arms

Here you have the disadvantage of not seeing the attacker. So you have to try to prepare your defense by shock or diversionary techniques. So you start by kicking backwards aiming at the foot or the leg of the attacker. At the same time you apply elbow strikes. The aggressor will loosen his grip. You take advantage of this by grabbing one or two fingers of the aggressor and pulling them suddenly to the side which causes a fracture. Now you can undo the chokehold, turn around and use fist punches, elbow strikes and kicks for defense.

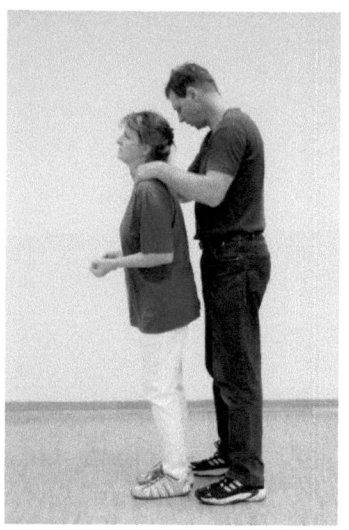 

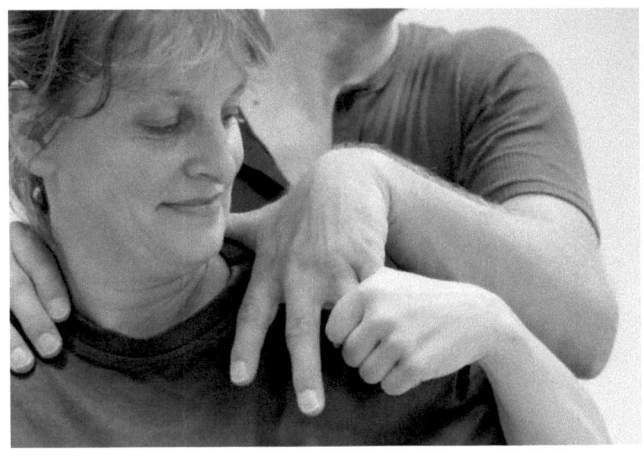

From behind with one arm

During such an attack the distance is so short that you can perform a backwards headbutt as your first technique of defense. Thereafter follow again kicks to the foot or the shin of the attacker. Then you grab one or two of his fingers and pull them all of a sudden to undo the chokehold like mentioned before. Afterwards follow the reliable fist punches and kicks.

Defense against headlock

You can use this defense against headlock from the front as well as headlock from behind. Here again we have a distance so short that it is no problem giving the genital area a fist punch. Before doing that you can use your other hand to pinch the attacker in his thigh as diversionary technique. After the punch to the genitals, again you grab one or two of his fingers and break them by pulling them suddenly to the side. Like this you free yourself effectively from the headlock. Here again – for your own safety - kicks and fist punches need to follow to disable the attacker with certainty.

Headlock from the front

Headlock from behind

Defense against a bear hug

From behind under your arms

First you do a backwards headbutt, kicks follow and at the
same time you hit the attacker's hands with your fists. Then
you loosen the grip by pulling one or two fingers suddenly to
the side. After you have freed yourself from the hug, you
"treat" the attacker to some kicks and fist punches.

From behind above your arms

First you perform a headbutt to the back and kicks. Then you loosen the hug by suddenly striking a "rider´s pose", i.e. you move your buttocks backwards and your stretched out arms forwards. Thereafter you loosen the hug through the above mentioned fracturing of the attacker´s finger or fingers. Then you kick him and punch him with your fist.

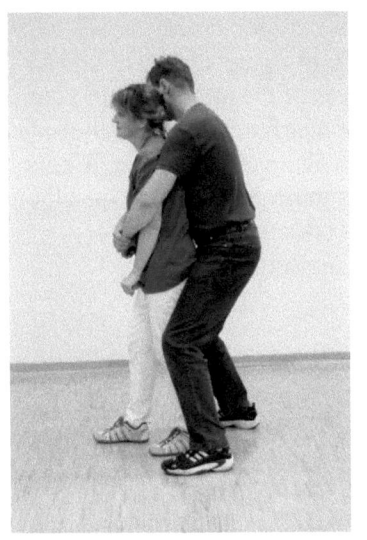 

From the front under your arms

Here you perform a forward headbutt to the aggressor´s head. Alternatively you may stab the eyes of the attacker with your fingers or thumbs. A fist punch or a strike with the heel of your hand to the attacker´s nose is also very effective. A knee strike to the genitals here also is a must. Strikes with the elbow to the aggressor´s head are just as effective. Then the aggressor will loosen the grip by himself.

From the front above your arms

First you only have the possibility to give the attacker a headbutt. Right after a knee strike to the genitals should follow. To prepare this it is recommendable to kick the attacker´s shin.

Defense from the ground

You may be as cautious and careful but it may still happen that you fall to the ground. This can have different causes, you may trip or the attacker pushes, pulls or throws you to the ground. In any case, the situation is still not hopeless. There are numerous techniques of defense you can apply from the seemingly worse position on the ground. To list them all would go beyond the scope of this book, so only a few selected ones are described.

First of all it is important and essential to roll yourself into supine or lateral position to keep the aggressor in sight and to take defensive measures. Lean on one of your forearms and keep the attacker with kicks at a distance. If necessary, you can change position by turning to the other side of your body or by turning on your buttocks.

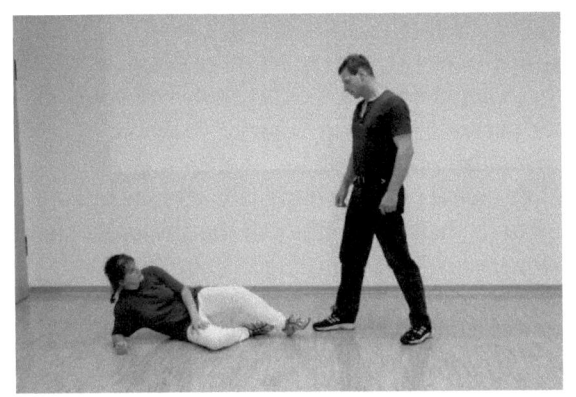

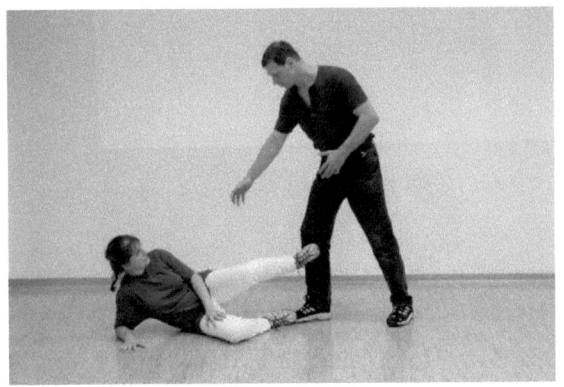

If this is not possible anymore and the attacker succeeds in grabbing you, try to get one leg (lower leg) between yourself and the aggressor to create a certain distance. Now the aggressor is so close that you can attack his face e.g. with strikes of the fist or elbow or with finger jabs into the eyes. Thereafter you grab the hair or shoulder of the abuser and pull him to the side with the help of your thigh. Your thigh will move from horizontal to vertical position. Through this lever action it is easier to tear the heavier man aside.

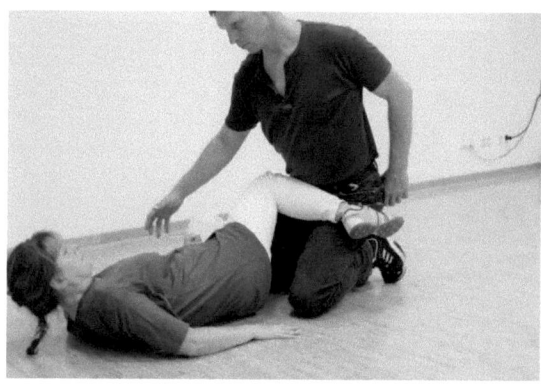

The following technique describes the case when you are not able anymore to get one leg between yourself and the attacker. Now the attacker is between your legs, bending over you. In such a case you can use the so-called "trunk squeeze", i.e. you put your legs around the hips of the man and cross them. Then you suddenly stretch out your legs. The result is that the kidneys of the attacker get squeezed which is really painful. But the trunk squeeze alone will not do for defense. You still need to strike the attacker's face with your fists (see previous technique). If the situation permits, you may strike the larynx which might however cause the aggressor's death. If you are not able to put your legs around the attacker's middle, you should kick your heels as often as possible into the attacker's kidneys.

Kicks

You distinguish a forward, sideward and backward kick. All kicks start alike. Of course it is important to keep your balance and not to fall over when you are performing a kick. That is why you slightly bend your knees before you kick this lowers the center of gravity and ensures a firm stand. You lift your leg until the thigh is in about a 90 degree angle to your body, your toes are lifted.

Starting position for all kicks:

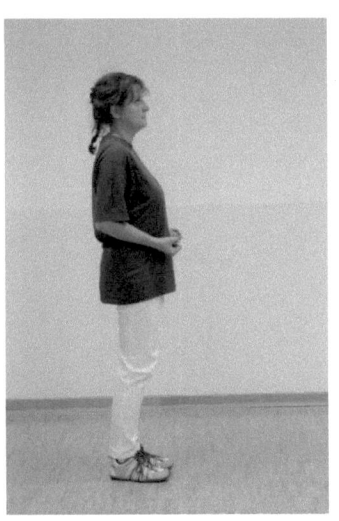 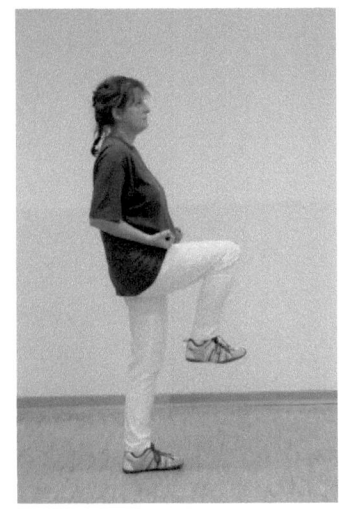

When you do a forward kick, you stretch your leg forward starting from this position. The ball of the foot is also turned forward whilst the lifted toes point backwards. So you do not kick with your toes but with your ball of foot. Then you pull your foot back into the starting position so that your opponent does not have the chance to grab your foot. He may very well unhinge you if the aggressor succeeds in grabbing your foot or leg. Moreover you drop your firm stand unnecessarily. Only after you pulled back your foot into the starting position you place your foot down on the ground.

For the kick to the side you stretch out your leg sidewards. The outside of the foot is the area with what you kick. When you kick you push your heel to the front and pull your toes backwards. Once you have finished this kick to the side you bring your leg back into starting position (a more or less 90 degree angle) and only thereafter you put your foot down on the ground.

The backwards kick is also being started from the 90 degree position. This time you kick with your heel i.e. you pull your toes direction of the knee. An essential element is the backwards turn of the direction of view, because you need to see where to you are kicking. Here also you bring your leg back into the 90 degree position before placing your foot on the ground.

You kick the so-called "low kick" in a semicircle or quadrant (not straight like the forward, sideward and backward kicks). You kick with your instep. Preferably you kick the back of the knee, the calf or the thigh of the offender.

Defense against kicks

There are different possibilities to defend a kick. In the following some of these defense techniques are explained.

You are in defense position. Your hands are clenched to fists, so that the arm muscles are flexed.

Defense from outside to inside

Through a lateral movement of your body you avoid the kick. The foot or leg is being parried with your forearm in a sideward movement form outside to inside towards the middle of the body.

Defense from inside to outside

Again you carry out the defense with your forearm, this time from inside to outside. Here you also have the possibility to take the attacker´s leg in to bend of your elbow right to unhinge him. This should take place right after defending the kick. In any case you should kick his genital area plus punch his nose or chin with your fist.

 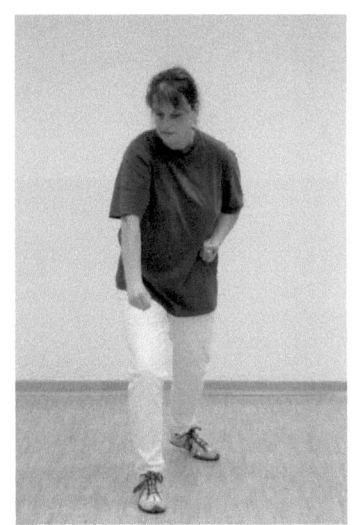

Defense with your own leg

For the defense now being described you need a certain amount of practice and a trained eye. You do not defend the kick with the arm but with the leg. The difficulty lies in finding the right moment for the defense.

You lift your leg in an angle of about 90 degrees and move it outside in a semicircle. Your foot is being put down immediately. Instantly thereafter follows the mandatory kick to the attacker´s genitals. As the distance to the aggressor is short, fist punches and elbow strikes are an effective method for the counter attack.

Acknowledgement

Several friends and acquaintances supported me in word and deed in the making and realization of this book.

I would like to say a warm thank you to:

Peter Denk
for all the hints and information, the editing, the patience and his inexhaustible knowledge of computers, with which he often gave me a helping hand.

Maribel Guzmán Neira
for the Spanish translation of this book

V. J. Herrera
for the English translation of this book

Detlef Sundermann
for the many tips and information and for the photos including the photo editing

Birgit Tron
for all the hints and suggestions

very special thanks go to my wife Marion
for being the defender on the photos, for the editing and for her limitless patience.

Without your help, this book would never have come into existence. You´re real experts! Thank you!

Contact to the author

If you want to contact Jens Müller to give hints, suggestions, praise or criticism, you can do this via:

Hajime-Selbstverteidigung@gmx.de

For more information visit the website:

www.Hajime-Selbstverteidigung.de

For your notes